7 Steps to Manifesting

YOUR DREAM LIFE

By

Michele Stans

———————

Proudly Published by:

Souptank Press - Nashville, TN 37221

Souptank Press, Paperback Edition 2017

Printed in the United States

This book is dedicated to the following:

My love and partner - Darren Christianson for supporting and loving me in all I do.

Both of my grandmas and Aunt Maria for guiding me in the ways of the Jedi.

My parents for accepting me as I am - even when it was a challenge.

My lightworker sisters who encourage and support me in so many ways.

My Life Coach and mentor Lin Church

My coaching professor, mentor, and constant support Dez Stephens and the whole Family at Radiant Health Institute.

(I know it's an Oscar speech but I tell my singers to sing like it's the last time so…)

To all my teachers and mentors that have supported and guided me to this place and beyond.

To all my Angels, Guides, and spirit level friends and family who help me every day.

And lastly to you, my reader friend. May this book be a blessing and a gift as it is intended.

Infinite love and gratitude,

Michele

CONTENTS

INTRODUCTION

"When you want something, all the universe

conspires in helping you to achieve it."

- Paulo Coelho

INTRODUCTION

Hi there! I am so glad you've chosen to invest in your dreams and to allow me to join you on this miraculous journey of yours!

In studying the Law of Attraction (LOA) for nearly three decades, I have seen and experienced so many fascinating examples of the LOA at work.

Most books on Law of Attraction include three vital and important steps:

1. Ask
2. Allow / Let Go
3. Receive

In my experience, I have noted a few more steps or characteristics in the Law of Attraction process that need to be added and applied to really get the Law of Attraction moving for us.

It is these steps I've learned, along with the three steps of Ask, Allow and Receive that I want to share with you here. I, for one, am so very certain of the Law of Attraction and how it has benefited me.

In the spirit of bringing evidence to the power of Law of Attraction, I want to share one of my personal LOA experiences that helped transform and deepen my faith in these exciting principles.

THE FLOOD

In 2010, the rivers and creeks around Nashville, Tennessee critically surpassed their 100-year flood levels. I don't live in a flood plain, but by noon of May, 2010 there was four feet of flood water in my home.

The very next day, we began to demo the first floor of our condo. When we were done, we could wave to our neighbors right through the walls, because there weren't any walls. There were just studs, electrical wires, some plumbing, and bits of left over insulation. The floors were stripped down to the concrete pad. It was surreal.

As I looked at the wreck my home had become, I realized I had no way of knowing how to fix this or if we even had a way of physically or financially making it right again.

I don't tell you this because I want you to feel badly for me. I show you this as my journey began here, like yours may be beginning today!

When we saw the water rising that morning, we packed our little family into two cars with all the necessities we could gather in about thirty minutes. As we sped away from the rising waters, I said emphatically to the Universe, "we are finding a place where we can regroup with our dog, RIGHT NOW!"

After trying to get to several friends' homes with no luck because the rising water had made most of the interstates and highways impassable, we found a hotel that had one (only ONE!) pet friendly room left. We took the room with a lot of gratitude.

The next morning I said to the Universe, "I know there is an apartment we can afford that will let us keep our dog, and allow us to be five minutes from our flooded home, so we can oversee reconstruction".

The next day, I signed a lease on an apartment that was exactly as I described, and even had views of a quiet park area, where we often saw deer and other animals grazing. This tiny apartment would become our sanctuary through the rebuilding process. However, despite our relative comfort, I began to wonder how we could keep going financially. I was wondering what happened to the part of the deal where I said, "an apartment we can afford".

We were paying both the mortgage on the flooded house and rent on the apartment. But, just as I was beginning to fret about it, a crazy miracle was thrown at us out of left field. As it turned out, when the company I worked for found out about our predicament, they graciously offered to pay our rent for the apartment, while we rebuilt our home. I'm still amazed and awed at this great gift.

Once our living arrangements were settled, we continued the demo of our home. This took only about a week and the only reason it got completed so fast was because so many friends began to show up to help. We didn't call, they just came. Two of my friends even came from Holland without any notice!

When the demo was over, I thought - where will we get the money to rebuild? Of course, we did receive help from FEMA that amounted to about $29,000. We knew that might get us through to installing the new HVAC, electric, gas and plumbing that needed to all be replaced, windows and maybe the insulation in the walls. However, it would not cover sheet rocking, floors, trim, paint or other finishes necessary to consider the house livable.I said, Universe I need some help here - I don't know how we're going to do this - so make a way.

Although it may be hard to believe, in only a few days we started receiving checks in the mail from people we knew, people we didn't know. People from ALL OVER THE WORLD! One friend even showed up with an envelope full of gift cards from her husband's work. There were yard sales in other states people held to raise money for us, and even a famous country singer held a benefit for us and others in our community. I had asked, I had allowed, and I had received. As amazing at these events sound, there's even more to this story that I'll share with you a little later.

I now live in a home that is beautiful in both style and energy, because it was built on love, gratitude, and the power of faith. I owe my situation to my understanding and application of the Law of Attraction. I now want to share it with you.

And, now it is your turn to experience the benefits of living within the Law of Attraction. What will your Law of Attraction story be? Let's start right now with a few exercises to get you thinking about what you really want, how to ask, how to be grateful, how to keep your faith, how to allow, and how to receive that which is already yours.

Chapter 1

GETTING CENTERED

"No one can be creative in a state of anxiety."

- Maria Nemeth

THE BEGINNING

How many times have you made a vision board, shouted to the Universe, or made lists of what you want, and then wondered why it didn't suddenly appear? I know I've found myself wondering this more than I'd like to admit. But I always remind myself that we are not waving some magic wand and zapping things into existence here. The Universe isn't our fairy godmother, it is our partner. We are co-creating our experiences with the Universe.

Take that thought in for a second. You may call "it" the Universe, God, or Higher Self. By whatever name, that same divine spark is within us and around all of us. When I think of it I sense just how big an honor it is to commune on the same level as divinity. Neat thought, huh?

Since that's kind of a big deal, it's interesting how sometimes we are so flippant about it. We take some paper and a glue stick, slap some pictures on poster board, with no real honoring of the time, the energy, or the good feelings those ideas might be bringing us.

We often forget the awesomeness of such moments. However, with some deliberate practice, these moments can become true moments of communion. Moments where we get a chance to deeply align our energies, our desires, and our intentions to that of the Universe. Getting into this powerful state of communion requires us to be centered and fully present to such moments.

We are a society that has come to expect immediate information or answers. Like some television sitcom that solves the family's problem in thirty minutes without any real work or deep reflection.

If we have an ache or pain and we want to cover it up by popping a pill, without thinking about the life choices that may be causing us this pain. We want it to move faster, download now, and keep us moving through our monkey brained existence. Yet, we still wonder why we are all so tired all the time, so disconnected, and even clueless about what we really want for ourselves.

So, how can we know what we want or don't want, if we don't take the time and space to know ourselves? In this module, that's what we are going to do. We are going to slow ourselves down a bit and get centered.

TURN OFF YOUR TV

If you want to know who you are and what you want, then stop allowing others to fill your brain with their ideas on how things "are" or worst yet, how they "should" be. How do you know what you want with the voices of others being pumped into your brain? We get these messages from the media in the morning when we get ready and in the evening before bed. Some of us allow ourselves to be exposed to this barrage all day long. I am not saying give up your favorite shows. Lord knows, I can't live without my

Downton Abbey. Well.. I can only watch reruns now, but you get my drift.

I am not saying, you should close yourself off from the world or stick your head in the sand. In fact, I would suggest that you might spend some time doing your own research on the news stories that trigger your interests.

The essential point: if you have other people's voices chattering at you all the time, how will you ever know your own voice? How will you know if the thoughts and feelings you have are really even yours?

So. I challenge you to take back the king or queendom that is your own mind-space. I challenge you to do it right now! No time like the present, and it is the present we are coming to right now. Plus, you might even save some money on that cable bill too.

GET HAPPY !

When you were a kid, what did you do for fun? Do you still do it now? Why or why not? You see, when we grow up and start taking care of all those "SHOULDS" and "obligations," we leave no space for the fun. One of my pivotal examples is when I became aware that despite the fact I was overweight, I couldn't name my favorite food. Now that is a problem. So, I'll ask you to answer these questions and once you answer them, I want you to go do them:

- What is your favorite hobby or pass time?
- What is your favorite movie?
- What is your favorite meal?
- What is your favorite album? (I know that's a hard one!)
- What is your favorite dessert?

It may take you five minutes or five days to answer these questions, but that's ok. Just go with your flow. Once you answer, do them each once - just to remind yourself what joy for you feels like.

A Note on Self Care and Self Love. Self-care is NOT selfish. It is a necessity for us humans to rejuvenate our energy every day. If we don't fill our cups with what brings us joy, how are we to be joyful in our relationships with others and those who we wish to help nurture?

"One cannot pour from an empty cup."

- Gandhi

MEDITATION

This one seems to be most challenging to folks and the most needed by the most challenged folks. Why? What are some of the issues people raise?

- I'm too busy to spend time meditating. (You need to meditate)
- I am too wound up to focus and meditate (You need to meditate)
- My mind won't stop whirring. (You need to meditate)

I can be pretty annoying with this stuff, huh? It's true that the folks who scream most about how they need to relax and connect are usually the ones making every excuse to avoid meditation or even taking a moment to be quiet. You get my drift… if you're saying "no" to this one, you most probably need to be saying "YES! YES! YES!"

Meditation doesn't necessarily mean sitting under a tree for an hour or seven, "OM-ing" your way to enlightenment. It can be as short as one minute or less.

It also doesn't have to be something you go at alone. There are so many great guided meditations. Some are for releasing different life stressors or just general relaxation. Some of my favorites start my day with focusing on my intentions. I love guided meditations, because they give us focus, direction, and provide a regulated way to get us quiet, present, and centered.

Many folks say their mind wanders too much. I'm here to tell you that it's OK. For instance, you might be meditating and suddenly realize you're making the grocery list. The good thing is that once you become aware of this type of thought, you can then mindfully bring your awareness back to your breath, to what the guide is saying, or to the music that you are focusing on.

The thing to remember is there is no blame in this game, no beating up of the self, just allowing yourself to be perfect in your humanity, and even grateful that you became aware of your thoughts, observed them, and took control of them. Bonus points for you!

Meditation can also be a great time to ask self a question. Think of what guidance you are looking for, and then quietly listen for the answer. I promise the answers will come.

Meditating puts you in the present. Our power is in the present moment, and being present is the foundation of attracting the life you want.

ACTION STEPS

Your exercises for this Getting Centered Module are centered (pardon the pun) around the discussed topics.

1) **Turn off the TV.** I am going to encourage you to turn off the news for one week. Grab the weather forecast from the internet. I follow my favorite weather guy on Instagram and he posts a quick forecast video each day or heck, grab the Weather Channel app, and get it that way. If you want to see what's going on in the world, try kicking it old school and read a newspaper. If there is show you love, then watch it. If you have Netflix or another streaming service, watch it there. There will be zero to few commercials, and doesn't that sound yummy!

2) **Do what brings you joy.**
   - What is your favorite hobby or pastime?
   - What is your favorite movie?
   - What is your favorite meal?
   - What is your favorite album? (I know that's a hard one!)
   - What is your favorite dessert?

Sit down in a quiet place and really think about these questions. Your answers need to solely be about you. No answer needs to be related to anyone else's needs. Only your likes, needs, and desires should be considered here.

This may take a bit and that's OK. It took me three days to figure out my favorite meal! Cray cray - right? Just peel that personal onion layer off and see what joyful things you can find in there.

Once you figure out your joy – Get out there and practice them. Eat that meal, watch that movie, listen to that album, etc. Write down how you feel afterwards. Try to find words more descriptive than "Good" to describe your feelings. Words like: elated, joyous, high flying, delicious, etc.

3) **Meditate.** I know… I know – you may have lots of reasons why not. So, I am going to excuse- proof this one for you. If you have a smart phone - download the app called: 50 One Minute Meditations by Robin Rice. It's free. Yep you can meditate in just one minute. I am going to encourage this as a daily practice. On YouTube, there are tons of great New Thought authors who have free meditations. All you need to do is search for them.

I am going to encourage you to search YouTube for a guided meditation by your favorite author and practice it each day for 14 days. Some suggestions are Wayne Dyer, Doreen Virtue, Marianne Williamson, and Davidji.

Get a meditation mala necklace. They are all the rage these days with the Boho look being so hip. I actually make them for folks with semi-precious stone crystals to enhance their meditation by connecting chakra energy through crystal energy.

For a beginner meditator, malas are super awesome, because they're a form of prayer bead. You might compare them to a Rosary.

To use a Mala: You have several beads in a row that are the same size. Each breath and/or mantra *(an affirmation or a chant that resonates with one of your energy chakras)* is one bead, then move to the next, and repeat all the way around the necklace.

Throughout the necklace there are usually larger or different shaped marker beads. These are there in the event your mind does wonder. When your fingers feel the change in the feel of the bead, it will remind you to bring your awareness gently back to the meditation practice. Once you get to the Guru Bead, you can either flip the necklace and go back around the way you came or end your meditation there. Before moving on to the next chapter, let's focus on getting centered and balanced. Let go of the things or ideas that don't serve you. Let go of any regret from the past or any worry over the future.

These thoughts and associated feelings are stealing your present moment. The present moment is where your life exists and where positive change can occur. So, are you with me? Let's take back our self-power by being present, centered, and fully in here.

Please, right now! Close your eyes. Take a deep belly breath in through the nose. Hold it for a count of 4 and then exhale, audibly, out the mouth for a count of 6. Focused on that breath moving? Good...let's begin manifesting.

Chapter 2

——

GRATITUDE

"The best way to show my gratitude is to accept everything, even my problems, with joy."

- Mother Teresa

THE FUEL OF LAW OF ATTRACTION

So now we are going to talk about an often overlooked element that really fuels the Law of Attraction process. The element is Gratitude. Some may ask, "What would I be grateful for, if I haven't even completed the "ASK" part in the Law of Attraction?" Furthermore, grateful for what? I haven't RECEIVED anything, because I haven't asked, yet.

That brings me to my AH HA point. You see…one does not begin receiving, just because we mindfully ask for things. In fact, you've been attracting everything in your life since your birth. Even at times when you weren't being mindful of what you were attracting. As we look carefully around our lives, we can recognize many things, people, and experiences for which we are grateful, and that the Universe has already conspired with us to place in our lives.

The concept of gratitude is actually a biggie. As you identify the things that make you happy in your life right now, the mere happy, grateful thought creates a higher vibration in you. Higher vibrations stir the pot of Law of Attraction, because like attracts like in the Universe. Happy thoughts attract and manifest more happy thoughts and experiences. It is the heart of the Law. In contrast to this idea, anxiety, fear, and negativity present as low vibration. The more you think and feel this way, the more your experience of life will reflect those feelings.

As Maria Nemeth said, "No one can be creative in a state of anxiety." This is so very true.

Try and think of a time when you created anything good in a state of anxiety? I can't remember any. That's why getting centered and exercising gratitude are such important additions to the process.

When we are in states of love, joy, or happiness, we present a much higher vibration to the Universe. As a medium, I can tell you that spirit guides, angels, and our spirit loved ones vibrate at different frequency levels from one another.

They definitely vibrate at a much higher frequency than most humans. The Universe or God vibrates at an even higher frequency than any of these. The closer we get to those levels of vibration, the more easily we co-create with the Universe.

To explain a little deeper, I'll use plants as an example. Plants vibrate at only a slightly lower frequency than our spirit friends. That is why we experience the feelings of both ethereal and grounding when we venture out into nature.

Plants are a great example of how gratitude works because seeds don't know how not to grow. They expand in the space they are provided and will happily use whatever space they are given.

If you plant a little seed, it innately knows to sprout and grow. You might say, the plant is thankful for the space it has been given. It grows into that space until it fills that space completely.

For example: You *(who are playing the part of the Universe in this scenario)* see a plant that has reached its full potential of growth in a small pot. If you want to see the plant expand, you'd need to give it a bigger pot. When you do re-pot your little plant, it will happily, and without thinking, bloom and grow into its new space. And so on. And so on.

It is the same with us humans, BUT there is a significant difference. The plants just trust in the process, while humans do not naturally respond in this way. You won't see a little seedling in the ground worrying like a character in a Woody Allen movie. The little seed doesn't worry about whether to sprout or to not sprout. The plant won't book an appointment with a therapist to discuss whether its blossom will be pretty enough or its fruit tasty enough. No - a plant doesn't know how not to flourish.

The good and the bad of being human is we have free will to make decisions and choices. We can choose joy or worry about expansion. When we choose joy we feel good, the Universe naturally provides us the resources and knowledge to fully expand and bloom. When we choose worry we fail to be grateful, disregard what has been provided, and ultimately push away our desires.

In short, the practice of Gratitude allows us to become aware of all that has been given and provided, and thereby we can gracefully use it for our growth and prosperity.

"Be thankful for what you have; you'll end up having more. If you concentrate on what you don't have, you will never, ever have enough." - Oprah Winfrey.

In gratitude, we find moments to remind self of our ability to work with the Universe in creating and manifesting wonderful things. We remember how we are not separate from it, but a unique vibration and manifestation of it. When we accept that we are the instigator, designer, and builder of ALL our happy, sad, or ugly life experiences, we expand our ability and knowledge of co-creation. Once we've gained this vital self-knowledge, we can never unknow it.

So... let's be grateful in all things, and let us commune with the Universe to let it know we are ready for some serious expansion.

GRATITUDE EXERCISES

Here are some exercises to try. Practice gratitude and feel the difference in your vibration.

1) BODY AWARENESS

Be very mindful of your thoughts and how your body feels when you think them. If you are worried or fearful - what's going on in the body? How does your body feel? If you are happy and joyful, what's going on in the body, and how does your body feel?

2) RELEASING

Release any fearful or worrisome thoughts by replacing them with gratitude. If you find yourself worrying about something bring your awareness to both the thought and the feeling.

Stop, breathe, and list in your mind three things you are grateful for in that very moment. If that is too difficult, think of your most loved person or pet to bring your center back. Hold onto that feeling of happiness and gratitude, as long as possible.

3) GRATITUDE JOURNALING

Buy a journal that is special for you. This will be your gratitude journal. Jot down three things you are thankfulfor as you are waking, and do the same before bed each night.

Don't skip it just because you had a bad day. In fact, these moments will clearly demonstrate the transformative power of gratitude. You can always find SOMETHING to be grateful for. For me, when nothing else pops, my go to gratitude item is "Indoor plumbing."

4) GRATITUDE VISITS

Is there someone in your life who has made a positive impact on you? Let them know. Sometimes you can set up a lunch date to take them to lunch to let them know. If they don't live close, maybe write them a REAL letter. Not just an email or a text, but a REAL honest to goodness, handwritten, pen to paper letter of your gratitude.

Let them know how they impacted your life and how grateful you are to them. Putting pen to paper makes things real for us. Also, remember how awesome it is to receive something in the mail that isn't a bill or an advertisement? A real letter - it makes you feel special. If all you have is someone's email, then of course that's OK too. Either way it is sure to not only raise your vibration, but raise that of another who you love.

Chapter 3

———

THE ASK

"Ask, and it shall be given you; seek, and ye shall find; knock, and it shall be opened unto you."

- Jesus of Nazareth

ABOUT ASKING

Let's recap a bit. In Chapter 1, we talked about getting centered. Some of my clients have asked, why getting centered and present was so important? My answer is always the same. Our personal power is always in the present moment. When we want to make a choice, manifest or connect with our highest levels of intuition, we will find our greatest power to do so in the present moment.

When we are in a state of regret or guilt about something, we are dwelling in the past. When we are worried or fearful, we are dwelling in an idea about the future.

There is no personal power in the past or the future. We cannot have any power in a place or time that doesn't exist in the now. The only place that our personal power is possible is right here and right now. I won't go into any technicalities of space/time continuum here, but I just want you to consider where your power exists.

Your power is in the present moment. Get centered, get present and be the superhero of your world. It happens in the right now. When we are centered and present, we are tuned in to the Universe and can begin co-creating together for the life we really want! Exciting!!!

In Chapter 2, we talked about gratitude. Gratitude is important because we are in a state of high vibration. One cannot be in gratitude and feel lack at the same time. To paraphrase Oprah, if you are seeing only what you don't have, you will never have enough.

When you are in present and in gratitude, you are being be open to receive more and more of that thing or feeling you are experiencing.

Gratitude = High Vibration

Lack = Low Vibration

The Universe is always vibrating at a very, very, very high level. To powerfully co-create what you desire - it's time to get some high vibe of your own going!

Even though Law of Attraction may not always work in the order I have put the steps, I put these two lessons first, because we want to prepare our minds and spirits with a high vibrational state, before we sit down to begin the process of manifesting anything. When we are centered and in gratitude, we know what we desire and are open to receiving.

There is no resistance to manifesting except for what we make. That said, as you go through this ask process, be sure to observe any limiting thoughts or beliefs. For instance, are you feeling guilt or fear about asking for you desires?

If so, then ask yourself why do I feel this way? Who told me I *shouldn't* want this? If the Universe / Source / God conspires to bring joy to me, then who am I trying to answer when I hear in my head that I *Shouldn't* want or do that?

Answering these questions will usually reveal all the different influences and definitions that have piled up in our minds from the others in our life. As we have passed through different phases of our life, we often have let the fears, guilt, and motivation of others become our own.

As we have grown up and out, some ideas in our brains helped us along the way. However, it's important to take stock when a thought or belief no longer serves us. It's much like operating a computer on outdated software. The software simply can't help us do the things we want to do anymore. It's time to upgrade.

We need to remember that everyone around us is on their own journey. They each have their own lessons and challenges to face. They most probably have no idea that the things they have said to us have replayed in our brain for years. They have no idea that our holding on to their beliefs of the world has been a detriment to our own journey. No need to blame them. They were doing their very best at the time.

UPDATING YOUR PROGRAMMING

Now that you are aware and present, you can decide and choose any new belief you want. Now, you can adopt beliefs and ideas that serve you on your personal path. It's all up to you now.

Two things about this to remember:

1) Everyone, including our parents, teachers, and elders, are on their own journey. Each is doing the best they know how in each moment. No matter how good or bad the behavior or belief might be.

2) Letting go of outdated "software" is OK. It may have been put there with "good" intention, but was installed with a kind of

   spiritual virus. In behavioral terms, we might say, installed by someone with personal motivations to shape your behavior.

Once you are aware of these thoughts, make sure you are thinking and doing things that support your own desired path. If your thoughts feel high vibrational, then you're on the right track. If there is wincing, low vibe feelings, or any generally icky feeling, then maybe this is something you need to address. Once identified, let it go with love and say no more to it.

"Accept no evidence other than your mood as important"

- Abraham Hicks

EMPOWERED ASKING EXERCISES

So on with "The Ask". This is where you decide what it is you desire. A Godiva chocolate bar? A new house or car? A life partner? A new pet? More time for self?

1) **Starting Small**

When you put an ASK out to the Universe, be specific as to what you desire. Stand in your power and ask. Start small like, I desire to see a pink car or wouldn't it be nice to have a breakfast sandwich - a sausage, egg, and cheese breakfast sammie! (I manifested a whole tray of these once - they were delicious!)

If you say something like, wouldn't it be nice to have breakfast brought to me - you might end up with a bowl of plain oatmeal, because you were ambiguous and the Universe is like oatmeal is healthy.

Some may like oatmeal, but I'd take my warm, comforting sausage, egg and cheese breakfast sammie over oatmeal any day.

2) Get Down to the Nitty Gritty (Write It Out)

Start thinking in detail about what you desire. What is it? What color is it? How big is it? What does it feel and/or taste like? How does it make you feel to have it? Really get clear on what it is you desire, so you can tell the Universe. Make sure the Universe and you are on the same page together in co-creating your desire.

Chapter 4

FAITH

"I have faith in the unlimited power of the Universe."

- Louise Hay

FAITH CHALLENGES

This is a quick, but very vital chapter on faith. We've talked about "the Ask" and some folks may find the asking exercises a challenge, while others have a monumental list ready to go!

This fourth step of faith may be a challenge to many folks. If you are like me, you may be a bit of a control freak. I confess, between being a Virgo and someone who has spent twenty plus years in the legal profession, I struggle often with control issues. Honestly, this is quite the challenge for me. I have found a few practices that have dramatically helped me with this issue, and I want to share them with you here.

"Everything you believe affected everything that comes to you."

- Abraham Hicks

LETTING GO

Much like in the movie "Frozen", I sing, "Let it go! Let it go!!" to myself on many occasions.

So... We've made our vision board, made our lists and all that other "Ask" stuff. I like to imagine the ask process like a drive-up bank lane, where we place our cylinders into that little sucky tube to send your deposits and withdrawal slips over to the teller.

In my mind, the Universe is the teller and we are placing deposits and making withdrawals from our own personal spiritual escrow account.

When we go to the bank, we fill out our little withdrawal slip, stick it in the cylinder, pop it in that vacuum contraption and press a button. A little door closes and ZOOM! Off goes the cylinder to the bank teller. Then the teller reads our slip, makes the requested withdrawal, and pops our cash back in the cylinder and ZOOM! It comes right back over to us.

So, I want you think about this process. Do we bug the teller? Do we micro manage this process at all? Do we worry the teller won't send it back to us? We know the teller is capable and that we have money in the bank to make the transaction. We have faith that this all works because it always does. We never question the process.

The Universe knows what to do when you show up at the "bank window" with your asks. This is where we usually get in the way, when we attempt to control how it gets done.

We know, if we send the little cylinder through the drive through, it WILL come back. If we plant a seed in good soil, it will grow. So, when you ask the Universe for something, imagine receiving it from that Universal teller. When we feel those beautiful feelings of knowing the process of manifesting is already worked out, we are resonating with our desire.

We are trusting in the Universal process, known to us as the Law of Attraction. When you resonate with your desire, you are giving the Universe a strong signal to release that desire from your spiritual escrow account. Like attracts like, remember?

"Be happy in the anticipation of what is coming." - Abraham Hicks

Remember my breakfast sammie story? I was at work and thought, "this oatmeal for breakfast isn't cutting it." I then thought, "It would be so fabulous, if I had a sausage, egg and cheese sandwich." Low and behold, fifteen minutes later our admin assistant came by my office and told me there was an extra tray of breakfast sandwiches from a morning meeting, and that we were more than welcome to have some. I wasn't a bit surprised that one of them was a sausage, egg, and cheese breakfast sammie for me! Voila and Yum!

THE "WOULDN'T IT BE NICE" GAME

Although my sandwich story sounds so easy, we humans like to try and control our happenings. I mean, why do we watch the weather report when we could alternatively just go outside?

So, faith may be a challenging task sometimes for us, but that doesn't mean we can't practice it often. In building your faith muscle, you might see it as a game. It's called the "wouldn't it be nice" game. Wouldn't it be nice to find $20? Wouldn't it be nice to get a free lunch? Wouldn't it be nice to win a vacation to __?

Just keep slinging your desires and intents out there and allow yourself to be open to receiving it. Ask with the expectation of it happening. I encourage you to do this and remember to stay in vibration with that which you desire. Like attracts like.

Just a quick note on language, as we will be going deeper into it in the next chapter. Our thoughts create what we say, and what we say becomes real for us. So, mind your words in this process and in Chapter 4 we will talk about why.

DAILY FAITH EXERCISES

1.   PLAY "WOULDN'T IT BE NICE"

To practice this, start small. Maybe intend, or set your Ask, for a certain type of car, or maybe a type of bird, maybe even intend for a small thing like a breakfast sandwich or a piece of cake (yep have done both and boy were they yummy!!)

Put yourself in a state of "Wouldn't it be nice if I received..." rather than a state of "I need..." Always resonating with the desire you wish to manifest. Then, JUST DON'T TRY to control HOW it might come to pass. Truly let it go. Maybe daydream about them, or imagine what it would feel like if you had them and then just let it go.

1) VISUALIZE AND FEEL YOUR ASK LIST

Look at your list of Asks - pick one and say, "Wouldn't it be nice..." Then close your eyes and imagine how it feels to have that. Linger on that. Be in the vibration of the joy you find when this comes to you.

2) WATCH YOUR MOUTH

Be very aware of your language when speaking of things you desire or don't want. Things to refrain from:

- I want
- I need
- I don't want that
- I hate that

These phrases and those like them resonate with lack and what it is you don't want. You're telling the Universe to pull these things to you. More lack and more of stuff you don't want.

Phrases that put us in vibration with what we desire:

- Wouldn't it be nice
- I am so grateful for
- Thank you, Universe for . . .
- I am so joyful that
- I am receiving
- I have…

These phrases and those like them raise vibration to that which we desire. Continue to practice positive phrasing around that which you desire before moving on to the next chapter.

Chapter 5

—

GETTING ALIGNED

"What the Universe will manifest when you are in alignment with it is a lot more interesting than what you try to manifest."

- Adyashanti

GETTING TRACTION

Don't worry, I am not sending you to the chiropractor. So far, we have seen that in order to get on the Law of Attraction train, we need to get centered, get an attitude of gratitude, really be clear on our "Asks," and let it go with faith to the Universe. BUT now what? We just don't stop thinking about our desires, do we?

Here's where vibration comes in. Everything and I mean everything in the known universe vibrates or resonates at different frequencies or speeds. Physics proves this fact for us.

Our words and thoughts even have vibrational frequency. For instance, if you say or sing the word "Love" it vibrates at a high frequency. If you sing or say the word "Fear", it vibrates at a low frequency. This is one more reason to be aware of the words we use.

Our words vibrate and move out into the Universe as our intentions. Those intentions either vibrate at a high frequency or a low one. The choice is ours.

Even if we are sarcastically speaking or using hyperbole like, "It's killing me!" How many times has this slipped out? Even when something isn't actually killing you?

More reasons to watch your words. They have power to manifest.

Back to vibration. I've mostly been talking about how to get and stay high vibe in figuring out and doing your "asking." Now, it's time to talk about getting and staying in high vibe as we learn to "let it go" or during that time where the Universe is doing its job in this process.

Remember when you completed your list of "wants" and then the feelings that would accompany those wants when they were achieved? Pull out that sheet because we are going to refer to it now.

Here's a little ditty from a man I adore. It's from Dr. Wayne Dyer on the subject of intention and manifesting.

"Act as if what you intend to manifest in life is already a reality. Eliminate thoughts of conditions, limitations, or the possibility of it not manifesting. If left undisturbed in your mind and in the mind of intention simultaneously, it will germinate into the physical world."

- Dr. Wayne Dyer

What this means is you'll want to act and feel as if you already have what you desire. Giving lip service about your intentions to the Universe does no one any good.

LISTENING TO YOUR BODY

But why, you ask. I made my lists, I made my vision boards, and I am saying my affirmations. My answer comes as a question back to you. Are you feeling them? When you look at your asks, do you feel them? When you look at your vision board, do you know these things are coming to you without any waiver in belief?

For example, when I say certain affirmations, I claim the heck out of them! I know them to be true. That's the easy part. When I say others, I feel my body twinge a little. Like, do I really believe that good thing about myself? And then I have a starting place as to addressing that twinge. We must be aware of those twinges first and have no fear in addressing them.

This is why we do the work to get centered and present. In this crazy world, we need to get back in touch with our bodies and how they respond to the world around us. We know when we feel good (high vibe) and when we feel bad (low vibe).

All that said, when we get to this point in the journey of manifesting we need to become aligned, vibrationally with what we desire.

LISTENING TO YOUR WORDS

Grab that Ask list now. Pick one of the things on the list. Now read the feeling which went along with it. That is the feeling which you need to align with to let the Universe know you are ready to receive it.

Here's a BIG secret. The Universe doesn't speak English, Spanish, German, French, Japanese or any other language spoken on earth. The Universe doesn't even speak mathematics, as some might suggest. The Universe's language is spoken in vibration, speed of vibrations and patterns of vibration. I know, you're probably thinking, "Michele - you crazy, girl!" Nope, about this subject, I'm completely serious.

Let me give you some examples....

- The person who claims they want a loving partner, but says all the time, "I only meet jerks." Where is their vibration? The vibration of their words and thoughts are not on Prince Charming, but on jerks. In resonating with the vibration of jerks, they'll only attract jerks.

- What about the lottery winners who end up in debt or worse? They put it out there that they wanted money, but their vibrations and words about money communicated somehow that they don't deserve it, that there is never enough money, or people will try to take this money from them. In thinking and speaking this way, they make themselves absolutely correct through the Law of Attraction.

□ What about the person who is so nice, sweet and kind, but always says things like, "Of course this would happen to me! I always have bad luck."

We might view these folks, and think how could such a nice person have such bad stuff happen? Well…it's because they chose to vibrate with it, resonate with it, and speak it into being.

What if the person looking for a life partner had said, "I am in a loving, caring, and passionate relationship with the perfect partner for me."

Isn't the point of all this to feel good, to be inspired, and to be in full alignment with our deepest desires. So, how do we get in this alignment, already? I will give you some more personal examples?

MY BEETLE BUG

I made a vision board of the VW beetle I wanted and made a declarative statement about it just about every day. I wasn't sure how I would receive this car, but I went about car shopping as if I did. I talked about my beetle as if it was in my drive way. I talked about all the things I liked about it, as I imagined it in my drive way. "My beetle is so cute & I am so cute in it!"

In just a few months of me aligning with my beetle this way, I received a brand new, perfect beetle, with all the bells and whistles, at a price I could easily afford AND with a few extras I hadn't expected. The Universe loves icing.

THE BIG FLOOD - PART II

As I mentioned earlier, in 2010, our house flooded in a city-wide flood. It took us 8 months and the love, financial support, and sweat of our friends, family, and community to rebuild our home. Near the end of reconstruction, we ran out of money and still had no staircase to the 2nd floor. We needed $5000 to get the project completed.

One morning, I went for a walk with my dog and said, "Universe, I don't know how it's going to happen but I need $5000 to buy all the stuff for the new staircase. I am going to leave this up to you. I am going to act as if it's already coming to us, because I know you're going to come through for me. Thank you."

After that I set about getting ready for work. When I got to work, I told my co-workers about the Downton Abbey-esque stair case I wanted, and how my Dad and boyfriend would put it in when the materials arrived. I talked about the color of the wood of my staircase and how pretty it would be.

So, at about 3pm that same afternoon, my phone rang. It was a local community organization that had been helping people whose homes had flood damage. They said … (wait for it), "We understand you may need some money to rebuild your home. We'd like to send you a check for $5000 to help you with your rebuilding efforts. Would that be okay with you?" No joke. True Story. Need I say more? And, yes, it was TOTALLY okay with me.

Notice the vibrations I put out in these two stories. I desired it with feeling, asked for it, and let it go to the Universe with gratitude, as if I had already received my desire.

It's the difference between being aligned with your desire and not. It's the difference between being in joy and being in resistance to your desires.

It is the difference between allowing the Universe to do its job and you saying, "Hey Universe - I got this," when indeed we cannot go it alone.

"What you Think… And what you Feel… And what Manifests is always a match. Every single time. No exception."

- Abraham (Esther Hicks as channel)

ALIGNMENT EXERCISES

1) **ASK WITH FEELING**
   Pick one thing on your list and sit quietly for 15 minutes. Close your eyes and imagine yourself receiving this "Ask". How does it feel? (expand beyond "good"). Dwell on that and how it expands in your awareness.

2) **EXPECT AND ACT WITH FEELING**
   If you are comfortable, tell a trusted and supportive friend about one of your "asks" and do so in the present tense. If you don't feel comfortable telling a friend - write it in a journal. Talk about how awesome it is to have your "Ask" arrive.

Chapter 6

AWARENESS & CONTRAST

"Awareness is the greatest agent of change."

- Eckhart Tolle

WAITING TO GROW

While we wait for our seeds to grow from the previous chapters, let's talk about contrast. By contrast I mean knowing what you do want and knowing what you don't want. This sounds simple on the surface, but when the contrast of what you want happens, it can be very challenging.

AWARENESS IN CONTRAST

For example, say you are in a job you just don't like. You are there every day. Your boss is a meanie, the environment is oppressive, and I could go on. You know you really REALLY want a new job. Now think about how great it is that you have this awful job. Say What!? Well stop and think about it. How would you know you want a new job, or maybe a new career, if you didn't have the current yucky job?

Similarly, if you're looking for a romantic partner and you think, "Gosh, I really don't like being single… and I really REALLY want someone to share my life with." How would you know you want a partner unless you were living a life without one, and furthermore, that you didn't like being without one?

We all have many experiences where we figure out what we do want by knowing what we don't want, but how does even that work, exactly? Easy peasy - it's how you are feeling.

The goal is to feel good, correct? Feeling bad, well feels bad or doesn't feel so good.

Now that you know you can choose everything right down to your thoughts, you can change this. The contrast allows you to know what feels good and what doesn't - its sole purpose is data and nothing more. A lot of times we get caught up in the feeling.

For instance, you drop your ice cream cone on the ground and you can either think, "Oh man, nothing EVER goes right for me. Like this or that other time…," dwell, dwell, dwell, stuck, stuck, stuck. Or it could be, "Bummer… hmmm - I wonder if the ice cream guy is still there and I can go get another one because those first couple licks tasted pretty good…" and off you go in search of what felt good. In that scenario, which feels better from a story reader point of view? The Debbie Downer version, or the *"OOH!* I wonder if there's more goodness where that came from?" Feeling good is the crux. Once we are feeling good - everything else is easy.

To turn up the contrast a bit, let's talk about high contrast situations where something shocking has happened. Maybe it is a sudden death of a loved one, a partner decides to leave, or maybe you get fired from work with no notice or reason.

In these high contrast moments, we normally have dramatic and sometimes irrational reactions to the extreme feelings of what we don't want.

It is in these experiences we can choose to fully embrace all we know about getting centered, present, calm, grateful, asking, knowing, and letting go.

AWARENESS OF ALIGNMENT (WHAT FITS)

I, Michele Stans, REALLY don't like Brussel sprouts. I discovered this at the tender age of 12. My mom made them for dinner and forced me to eat at least one, even though the smell of them alone nearly had me under the table. I tried the one, and then and there I decided, quite emphatically, I did not like them at all. From that moment on, I never ate a Brussel sprout again.

Why wouldn't I eat them again? Because they - to me - are gross! The taste to me is a little past horrible, the smell sour and disturbing, and I can't even have them cooked in my house, because their smell lingers. Why would I ever put myself through that again? That's just it - I don't and I won't do it again. It doesn't feel good!

I am sure there is a food you *really* don't like. You don't like it, you don't buy it, you don't make it for yourself, and you certainly would never choose to eat it. Why? Because you don't like how it tastes or how it makes you feel.

Keeping that idea in mind… We all have experiences with people, work, places, and things we don't like. However, unlike the food example, we choose to feed ourselves with these things over and over and over again. Sometimes, we make these things our diet almost every day.

The "why" of why we do this to ourselves is a whole other book. However, I can say here that it all boils down to one thing, and that thing is our ability to self-love. So, ask yourself, "Do I love myself enough to know I deserve the best?" What is your answer? Regardless of your answer, repeat after me:

"I deserve the best and I accept the best now!" "I love and approve of myself!" - Louise Hay

Please, repeat this at least 10x a day. For some of you it may take a little time to get used to saying to yourself, but I promise you'll like the benefits of doing it. In this simple affirmation, you will begin to make different choices. You will start releasing resistance to the things you want and align with them. So, be aware of what you are allowing into your life experience. It is all a choice, whether you "choose" to recognize that fact or not.

AWARENESS OF YOUR LANGUAGE

As we discussed in Chapter 5, even though the Universe doesn't communicate via language or words, it does communicate in levels of vibration. Words are the expression of our thoughts. So, it is really important that you pay attention to your words, and even the tone in which you deliver them.

When you speak are you being sarcastic, bombastic or using hyperbole? Do you say things like, "This cold is killing me!" or maybe "I can't wait!" These statements and the vibrations in them are telling the Universe where you are putting your attention and awareness vibrationally, and it kindly sends it back to you, as you requested.

Louise Hay is the queen of affirmations in my book. So I will share and paraphrase some of hers here. Affirmations are a great way to train the mind and your vibration into heading in the direction you want to go.

Are you not happy with your job?

I bless my current job with love and release my current job with love. I now create a wonderful new job for myself where I am valued and appreciated. I work for and with people I love, in lovely environments, and am paid very well for my work.

58

Are you trying to lose weight?

I love myself just as I am. I am beautiful and everybody loves me. I am eating healthy foods and drinking healthy beverages.

I am releasing this wall of excess weight. I am safe and I am divinely protected.

Are you looking for a partner or maybe want to patch up a quarrel with a family member or friend?

I have wonderful and harmonious relationships.

Do you see how we phrase the desires in present terms, positive ways, and focusing ONLY on the desired outcome?

Let's start rephrasing your thoughts and words to, "My body functions at its best every day!" or "I am so looking forward to _____." These kinds of statements bring your vibration to that of wellness, happiness and even joy. These kinds of vibrations and statements are the opposite of the contrast you may have been and/or are currently experiencing.

In doing this small adjustment of thought and language, you will be aligning yourself to your desires. In aligning yourself with your desires, you allow the Universe to manifest them for you at the perfect time and space.

As you begin to see your desires align with you through the Law of Attraction more rapidly, it will be a sign to you that you are learning the lessons of your life's journey. As you more expertly implement the Law of Attraction, the Universe will open up to you.

"When you change the way you look at things, the things you look at change."

- Wayne Dyer

AWARENESS EXERCISES

1) **Word Phrasing**

   Phrase everything from where you want to be not where you are or don't want to be.

2) **Do Affirmations**

   Google - Louise Hay Affirmations and then click on images and find some that resonate with you and write them down in your journal. Then say them 10x a day for a week.

3) Practice Awareness of low vibrational word use

Start being aware of when you are focusing on what you don't want. When you become aware of your focusing on what you don't want, just say to self, "This is just data and I can easily refocus on what I do want."

4) Continue listing points of Gratitude

Make a list of all the things you love about your life right now in your journal.

5) Parking Spot Pickup Game:

When going to the store, imagine you getting a parking spot in the perfect place as you are driving there. What does that feel like? Focus on that. Don't Think - FEEL!

Chapter 7

———

THE ART OF RECEIVING GRACEFULLY

"The greatest gift you can give another person is to gracefully receive whatever it is they want to give us."

- Fred Rogers (Mr. Rogers)

TIME TO RECEIVE

In the preceding chapters, you have learned the importance of being centered and present, being in a state of gratitude, the importance of knowing what you want, asking with feeling and elevated vibration, and the vital step of letting go to the Universe.

You've also explored the subtle, but powerful nuances in language, levels of vibration, living with contrast, as a constant teacher, self-love and putting your awareness toward what you really want.

We've arrived at our last chapter and our last step in the Law of Attraction. All that is left is to receive those desires in manifested form.

THE UNIVERSE IS KNOCKING

You've done all you need to do and the Universe is ringing your doorbell, because it has left your package on your front porch. Do you open the door or stand there looking at the door? Are you debating with the old voices about what might be on the other side of the door? Those old voices might be running the below questions by you, as you stare at the door…

- Am I really worthy?
- Do I deserve what I asked for?

- What will people think when they see I've received what I asked for?
- Will people judge me for pursuing what I want?
- My family always said, "I need to live humbly and not be showy."
- I am afraid this will be too difficult.
- People who always get what they want have a sense of entitlement.
- People who prosper seem to be mean and I don't want to be like that.

Any of these old voices sound familiar? Have you ever asked for something, and when the thought of receiving it came, you began to list all the strings that would be attached?

You can admit it quietly to yourself, if you ever have such thought patterns. No worries. I won't tell and honestly there's no shame in it because once you address it, it's not hidden anymore.

How well do you take a compliment? When someone says to you, "That outfit looks great on you!" or "You look fabulous!" Do you reply with, "This old thing?" or "Really?" Why is it so difficult for us to just say "Thank you so much!" Why won't we just enjoy the good feeling?

The answer to why, is our old software programming once again. Whether it's receiving something small like a compliment or big like a lottery win, we seem to have lots of interesting ways of speaking and thinking about it.

Most of our thoughts in these situations don't serve us one bit. The part of our old programming that seems to be the faultiest is the part that says we SHOULD be humble, self-deprecating, and selfless whenever anything good is presented.

Usually, if we find ourselves muting our reactions to gifts of compliments or things, we are out of alignment with Universal Law of Attraction. When we choose to do this, two specific things have definitely occurred.

1) **THE ITTY BITTY @#!*#! COMMITTEE / OLD PROGRAMMING WINS AGAIN**
   The itty bitty (you know what) committee chimes in saying, "Rein it in buckaroo. Nobody likes a conceited person!" And you reply, "Oh yeah…" and spurt out "This ol' thing? It's been in the back of my closet. I never thought it was flattering."

2) **REFUSAL OF POSITIVE ENERGY FLOW**
   When a person gives a compliment or a gift, they are sending positive energy to you.

When you choose not to receive the compliment or gift, you are disallowing that positive flow of energy to you, and are not reciprocating positive energy flow in the form of a simple thank you. Without this exchange, the opportunity is lost to raise everyone's vibrational frequency.

YOUR NEW PROGRAMMING

My friends, please, declare with me, right now: "I choose to release all the programing that no longer serves me! I now accept and receive compliments, gifts and awards from people and the Universe with love and gratitude!" THANK YOU!

From this new place, here is the compliment scenario revised… A friend says, "Wow - that outfit looks fabulous on you!" Your response: "Thank you!"

You now are receiving the positive flow of energy from your friend and reciprocating by saying thank you. It is a statement of gratitude and you and your friend receive an elevation in your vibrational frequency.

Now, apply this to a bigger picture. You meditate a little to get centered. Part of your meditation is focused on affirming the gratitude you have for your current car. You bless your car with love and know that you will release this car to the next person to drive it with ease and love.

You open your eyes from your meditation and start a vision board. On your vision board, you put pictures of your dream car. You glue on an affirmation that says, "I now create a wonderful new car for myself. It is a _____, and is in a beautiful color for me. The experience of receiving this car is easy and flowing, and it comes to me at a price I can easily afford. All of this or better. I receive it with gratitude and love."

Then, two days later, you see the car on the Internet at your local dealer and holy moly it's at the best price ever and in a color you never knew you loved!

When you get to the dealership, there are two cars pulled to the front door waiting specifically for you. The one you saw on the website and another that is newer, better warrantied and with a bunch of cool bonus features. It's much better than the one you found on the Internet....AND... it's cheaper!

You trade your vehicle for more than you thought possible, the deal goes so smoothly you can't remember a better transaction, and at last, you drive home in gratitude to the Universe for sending you such an awesome deal!

Sounds a little too easy? Well . . . It took me two years to get there, but now I drive my dream car. I love the VW Beetle that now sits in my driveway. So. Why did it take me two years to find it?

Well…It took me two years of hemming and hawing around about what exactly I wanted. However, when I sat myself down and got specific, practiced what I preach, and let go of the details of the "how", it was very little time at all.

Please, whatever you do, release the old, out dated programming that says you are not deserving, that says you are not worthy, and says people who get what they want are "bad". Release all these judgments and programming.

Think about it, who are you answering to in these imaginary situations? In these conversations? Is it your mom and dad? Teacher from the 4th grade? Some random person you overheard in the grocery line commenting on a tabloid story? Nope…You are answering to yourself.

If you listen to the voices and repeat them over and over, you stop yourself from feeling good, from being happy, and receiving your good. If you reprogram your internal voices to be supportive and loving, then you are still answering to yourself, but in a way that moves you toward what you want and your highest good.

If you've been living with old programming for years and nothing seems to be working out the way you want, then maybe if you try these practices - something will. It can't hurt you. It doesn't cost a thing to imagine what you want, be grateful for you have, ask and expect in states of high vibration, and receive good things with grace and gratitude.

If you get nothing else out of this book, please know you are divinely loved. We were not created to suffer and be in states of unhappiness. We were created to be in joy and to shine our light on others.

RECEIVE THE BLESSING

So, my friend, with my full attention, intention, and gratitude, I leave you with this final thought from me.

Know that I am so very grateful for you. I ask that my words be a great blessing to you, and that you allow yourself to fully receive all the desires of your heart. All this and better I ask for you from the Universe.

Now it's up to you. Do you receive this blessing? What say you?

Namaste,

Michele

ABOUT THE AUTHOR

Michele Stans is a Certified Holistic Life Coach. She specializes in law of attraction, self-empowerment, and intuitive training. She is a Master Intuitive Angel Tarot Card Reader.

Growing up in New York helped shape Michele's humorous, authentic and direct form of communication. Whether speaking to her clients or her spirit guides you can always count on Michele to speak compassionate truth into a situation.

Her intuitive gifts started early, and she learned the intricacies of talking with the angels and spirits under the loving mentorship of her grandmother and aunt. Now, with more than thirty years of experience working with clients, Michele enjoys helping others find their answers.

Michele refers to her unique approach to life coaching and intuitive practice as, "soul coaching." Through her work, Michele helps her clients not only access the answers they are seeking, but shows them how to rediscover what their soul already knows.

Whether her clients want help understanding their life path, figuring out a relationship, or just curious about what the angels want for them, right now, a "soul coach" session with Michele improves their sense of balance, purpose, and self.

She is currently living in Nashville, Tennessee, where she works with her ever growing list of "Soul Coaching" Clients.

Certifications and Memberships:

~VP and founding member of the Ladies of Light Sisterhood

(chapters in Nashville, Atlanta, and the United Kingdom)

~Certified Holistic Life Coach

~Certified Angel Card Reader

~Certified in Chakra Wisdom

~Certified in Life Force Energy Healing

Contact:

www.soulcoachstudio.com

email - soulcoachstudio@gmail.com

Facebook - www.fb.com/soulcoachstudio

Twitter & Instagram - @soulcoachstudio

www.ingramcontent.com/pod-product-compliance
Lightning Source LLC
Chambersburg PA
CBHW031525040426
42445CB00009B/402